Terry Quinn

Notes on the Causes of
The Third World War
by
J C Dunne

Indigo Dreams Publishing

First Edition: Notes on the Causes of The Third World War
by J C Dunne

First published in Great Britain in 2020 by:
Indigo Dreams Publishing
24, Forest Houses
Cookworthy Moor
Halwill
Beaworthy
Devon
EX21 5UU
www.indigodreams.co.uk

ISBN 978-1-912876-43-3

British Library Cataloguing in Publication Data. A CIP record for this book can be obtained from the British Library.

Designed and typeset in Palatino Linotype by Indigo Dreams.
Cover design from artwork by Jane Burn.
Printed and bound in Great Britain by 4edge Ltd.

Papers used by Indigo Dreams are recyclable products made from wood grown in sustainable forests following the guidance of the Forest Stewardship Council.

to
Julie Maclean

Acknowledgements

I would like to thank Judy Brown for reading a draft of this pamphlet and for her insightful comments, notes and advice that pointed the way forward for me.

CONTENTS

Foreword

In the immediate aftermath
of any armed conflict
there is an understandable rush
to put into place words and images
in an often confusing period.

Even I was guilty of succumbing twice
to the lure of a guaranteed headline
and a hefty addition
to an academic's bank balance.

But enough time has passed
and, more importantly,
papers and minutes have been released,
one way or another,
that now gives an opportunity
for a formal objective study,
not of the war itself
that will come later
and requires far more space
than this brief pamphlet

but in the meantime I feel
that there is a need to examine
some of the elements of that period prior
to when the world broke down.

Introduction

I am an historian,
I like facts,
I like reasons
backed by evidence
for the actions
or inactions
of humans in reaction
to whatever events
are being studied.

Which is splendidly objective
but completely ignores
that I have been affected,
I have seen history,
been part of it.

I am a winner
that has lost
like all of us here
so if I let slip a hint of bias
then that is my fault alone.

A Question of Time

I am writing these words
during long light hours
but when I was a child,
and my undergraduate students
do have difficulty with this,
in the city of Birmingham
on the midland's plain of Britain,
then my homework
was done in the evening,
the day was for playing,
swimming in pools
or football until it got dark.

Which may seem an odd introduction
to the causes of a war
but let's look at those statements
a little more closely.

I could work at night
because energy was abundant,
we grew and grew
shot up with chemicals
and Gross Domestic Product,
growth was as natural as sunlight,
diseases were always beaten.

As my colleague, Dr Teresa Danby,
so elegantly puts it,
we got to the point
where our heads were in sand
and our backsides in clouds.

And who knows
maybe the children I see
through my window

in the school opposite
will grow like us.

They're playing the same games
running and screaming in their break
not a care in the world
their world
and we mustn't forget that.

A Present from the Past

There is a Professor of Glaciology
at this University
who starts her first lecture
to a fresh intake of students thus:

Lock the door and don't move.
I mean it.
This stuff melts, even here,
I'd hate to see your grants cancelled.

And then she slowly,
some may say dramatically,
removes insulation
from a long slim column of ice
drilled from a glacier
that once covered
where these words are being written.

She's told me,
many times,
that the most common question
in the Refectory later
is why those cores
were ignored.

Crossing the Line

We raced to eight billion
what country would win,
which mother, whose baby,
the media loved playing with words

but not with the fact
that as temperature rises
so does pressure

I have no idea
how many letters were signed
by concerned citizens like me
who never understood chemistry
but could see it happening
as people started to escape
the sort of pressure
I could understand
in a professional capacity

but I didn't foresee
what was to follow.

A Legacy of the Last Century

One of the treasures
I managed to grab,
before being evacuated,
was a handmade quilt
patches of different colours
sewn by my mother's mother.

It fulfils its purpose
but in addition,
in a certain light,
in a certain mood,
its blues, greens and whites
remind me of Earth
as it used to be.

And from this new vantage point,
both literally and figuratively,
I can make out threads
unstitched over the years
flaccid poles
flagging the end of what we knew.

Nationalism, Communism, Capitalism,
primary types of isms.

I called them Prisms
in some text book or other,
a term I was rather pleased with,
which seems to have caught on,
with its hints of refracting
what was happening beneath the covers.

A View from Above

There is a photo
taken from the Space Station.
I have it on my office wall,
it shows a night time planet
when city lights
twinkled around the globe.

We had a game
join the dots
the quickest   the shortest
the most interesting way
to get from, for instance,
Nairobi to Oslo
my wife decided who won.

I remember the furore
when the crew updated it
posting Earth divided
by a broad black band
either side of the Equator
and called it The Third's World.

My wife didn't think it was funny.

The Assassinations

It does not fall within the compass
of thin or thick books of history
to make moral judgements.

Squeezed between
the full stops and commas
it will be inevitable
that there will be
a slight colour here
a suggestion there.

And I'm putting that disclaimer in now
as it's time to mention that brief period
when the political classes
were targeted in Chile, Sweden,
the United States and Germany.

One of the oddest aspects
of that wave of bombing and shooting
was that it was the most law abiding citizens
who had weighed the evidence
of science versus political inertia
and had decided to act
in the name of the greater good.

Now, with twenty-twenty hindsight,
they were, of course, irrelevant,
at best questions were raised,
at worst they gave governments
absolute power to do absolutely nothing,
but, in quiet moments, I sometimes ask,
well, what would I have done.

Lost

There is the famous image
of the first island overwhelmed

a single flag flying

seas breaking the top floor
of a civic building

and the face of a child
cleverly caught
sitting alone
on the deck of a lifeboat
not understanding

and the same face
coming ashore
to welcoming crowds
in a big city
even I had to check where it was.

The Need for Documentation

Current research,
at this University,
suggests migration patterns
were not as clear cut as first supposed.

For instance, West African people,
or what was left of them,
were indeed halted
by the Las Palmas Blockade
but more got through
than was reported at the time,
just check the dead
at the Battle of Bilbao.

There are too many of these quirks
to be included in this study
and given the lack of records
from parts of the world
that no longer exist
in any meaningful way
it may only be word of mouth
that eventually reaches
some sort of conclusion,
but I'm not holding my breath.

The Antarctic Solution

The transfer of migrants,
through Tierra del Fuego,
was not, as it happens, planned.

This may raise a few eyebrows
in some far flung places
but it is quite clear
that the sudden arrival
of around 5 million refugees
from countries
on the Tropic of Capricorn
took governments to its south by surprise.

It was, of all things,
the preparations for a football World Cup
that meant that materials
including food and drink
were ready at hand
to transfer migrants quickly
to refugee camps constructed
on the then little known Palmer Land.

Whether this was undertaken
in a ruthless or selfless manner
still depends, I'm afraid,
on your point of view.

A Defensive Strategy

It is now clear that the islands
north of Australia
had well established plans for partial evacuation
when certain trigger points were reached.
We don't know, as yet, what those points were
but almost certainly were related
to temperature and rioting.

Those who were allowed to leave,
at a best guess of 3 million
based on pre-war population figures,
obviously headed south
where after initial successes
in landing on Bonaparte Gulf
and the Cape York Peninsula,
came to the killing grounds
of already uninhabitable deserts
in the central part of that continent.

The few who did get through
and the thousands who tried
to round the coasts
met a different problem.

One paper which has emerged
since starting to write these notes
is on the discovery of the original document
from the Prime Minister's Office
which foresaw some of this happening.

Ironically, given the space in Australia
and to a lesser extent New Zealand,
it was the use of walls
that led to the success,

if that is the right word,
in keeping much of the original population
remarkably untouched
after these initial
and short lived pincer movements.

How and when they go about
removing these walls
will be interesting.

Developments in the North

The almost unbelievable act,
at the time,
of demilitarising the Bering Strait
puzzled many people
and still puzzles some people.

Perhaps it may help younger readers
to understand this
if I tell of a chance meeting
my wife and I had with an American teenager
when we were youth hostelling in Spain
and he refused to believe
that Russia and America
were only three miles apart.

The recent discovery of minutes
taken at the Aleutian Conference
make it clear that all parties
thought it would ease pressures
on their own lands
and push millions into areas
that were then so remote
but so politically charged
that removing the barriers
had the added advantage
of sending a message
that old enmities were gone.

The relative isolation
of Greenland and Iceland
in the build up to conflict
is partially explained
by their lack of land borders
and highly effective naval defences.

On mainland Europe
the fear of war was deeply ingrained
and political structures had evolved
to avoid yet another war
but thirty million refugees
and the certainty of many more to follow
took its toll on pity and resources.

A Digression

Far more people died
during the period of conflict
from drought and starvation
than from acts of war.

For instance
the virtual eradication of Bangladesh
and most of its population
due to crop failure as a result of rising sea levels
had been expected for so long
that it barely made the news.

I've checked the records
and coverage of the decrease
in flow of the Indus
was barely mentioned
outside the Asian Subcontinent.

There was more coverage
of water shortages in Cape Town.
To the return of the dust bowls
in the North American midwest.
Many of us will remember the shock
when Perth was abandoned.

Questions are starting to be asked
as to why people like me
have never addressed the implications
of this lack of coverage
but that is a separate question
and did not affect the course of the war
in any meaningful way.

Beginnings

I don't know where it was proved
but most accidents are caused
not by one mistake
but by a combination of circumstances
not all of them obvious
even now
but here are a few
in one small part of the world
that proves the point.

The population of Khartoum fleeing
the hottest summer on record,
the failure of wheat crops in Afghanistan,
and cholera in Tobruk.

But no one really expected
that a confrontation might take place
so the announcement that
the 1st Battle Group of the Persian Army
had been formed as a result
was treated, initially, with some derision.

However, there were many
small parts of the world
many mistakes
and the circumstances combined.

The Tromso Agreement

It's a commonplace
to put the signing
of the first Polar Treaty
as a sort of Chamberlain moment,
pieces of paper flying
in the face of reality
as politicians waved to their crowds
while the ice melted
faster than ink
drying on the pages.

With respect,
that wasn't the point,
it was the buying of time
and the selling of hope
and let's face it,
what the hell
are we doing now?

My Enemy's Enemy

Trying to make sense
out of the shifting allegiances
just up to the outbreak
of the first months of the conflicts
is a problem not just confined
to students, politicians
and the casual reader.

It would, indeed, be a surprise
if a month went by
without some memo being found
that indicates that the old maxim
about enemies and friends
is true but not necessarily
for any length of time
or on the same continent.

I have a doctoral candidate
researching this very subject
and the results, so far,
have been interesting as to
the fluidity of various factions
up to the outbreak of formal hostilities.

On the North American Continent

When news of the ironically termed
Battle of Stalingrad
reached the mid west,
and more importantly
the coastal strips
of the North American Continent,
the disparate groups from its central belt
coalesced remarkably quickly
under the leadership
of previously unknown names
from drugs cartels prevalent at that time.

There is no need for more words
on that subject,
some people have found it fascinating,
but what is becoming clearer
from priests released from their vows
is the role that the Roman Catholic Church played
in mediating behind the scenes
both before and crucially after
the moving of the Apostolic Seat,
but suffice it to say here
that, surprisingly, it was only in that region
that religion was a factor
in the opening of a battle front.

Failings in Europe

Because of the relatively bloodless stalemate
of the Mongolian Front
it has received little attention,
but I would argue that
the deploying of the then
newly formed Baltic Division
had a decisive effect
on the rest of European defence strategy
to the extent that the Pyrenean line
was fatally compromised.

If that's heresy
in the light of subsequent events
then I plead guilty.

But I must remind you
that even at this late stage
it was expected,
by governments and their people,
that diplomacy combined
with the rattling of armoured brigades
would prevent the unthinkable.

But that also meant not thinking
about the absolute need
for large parts of the world
to escape, at best,
extreme living conditions
and, at worst, certain death,
so, what did that world have to lose?

A Misunderstanding

The Battle of Stalingrad
had all the hallmarks
of what constitutes a major confrontation,
but it was by no means
the start of a World War
and this is a point
that previous commentators
have, quite simply, got wrong.

It was, in fact, seen at the time,
even in the irony of its title,
as the end of the threat of potential conflict,
the images shocked continents,
there were demonstrations
in all the major cities,
you can still see the graffiti
in what's left of some of them.

My wife was in Bruges
and brought back a poster
black background and pale blue dot
no words
she just looked at me.

The Final Days of Peace

Once again I'll spell it out

there was no single reason
for the final disintegration into war.

I'm not going to reveal
some startling new facts,
rabbits out of a hat,
that show that there was
some sort of definitive moment,
that suddenly changed the world
from a state of peace to a state of war
and at a stroke
change our perceptions and memories.

It's not going to happen.

The best analogy I've come across
is made by Dr Martinsen
of the University of Stavanger
who described a gradual transition,
like a cluster of bushfires
that slowly amalgamated.

However, in all the subsequent
and individual confrontations
there were a few that stand out.

One was the taking of the Grand Coulee Dam
by an unexpected advance
from what would become the 3rd Brigade
of the Coalition's Pacific Division,
one was Shanghai being lost to fire,
one was the collapse of the Saudi oil field.

The only thing that I can add to this
is to fit another piece of a jigsaw,
the time when I finally knew it was too late,
and that was when Ireland
was forced to break its neutrality
and there was only one place left to go.

The Bombs

that weren't used.

But it was close
and it's the one subject
that I do agree on
with all of my professional colleagues.

Readers will be aware
of the collaboration between us
in what is the definitive work
Nuclear Weapons – Nein Danke

We have been criticized
for the flippant title
but I, we, stick by it
as much for our sense of relief
as anything more profound.

If I can sum up
five hundred and thirty six pages
into four lines of why
those weapons were not used
they are:
incompetence,
a refusal to obey orders,
the deaths of key technicians
and sheer bloody luck.

A Personal Statement

I have tried
and mostly succeeded
in keeping this work
within an academic discipline
but these rules, although useful,
belong to a world that has gone.

I am no detached third party,
none of us are now,
so I want to write about Maggie
my wife Maggie
although everyone reading this
will have their own reason
for keeping their own story alive.

Staff Nurse Dunne
who agreed with me
when I couldn't see the point
in being a part of that present

who packed my case
who waved me off
the last boat from Galway

she wasn't for the fighting
no side was worth it
that's what she said
but I can change a bandage
that's what she said
as she gave me an envelope
her last will and testament.
I'll never open it.

Epilogue

A colleague asked me
how many types of government
there'd been in history before now,
she's a mathematician
so I don't know why,
but for simplicity and a quiet life
I ignored Plato
and gave her City States, Empires
and the Nation State.

She could argue,
well, I would,
that mass communication
did for the first two
which left Nation States
at the turn of this century
as, more or less, the status quo.

But that was then
and now we're in the state we're in,
something untried and untested,

And that's the interesting thing about history.
The future.

Also by Terry Quinn

away (Poetry Monthly Press), 2010.

The Amen of Knowledge (Indigo Dreams Publishing), 2013.

To Have to Follow (Indigo Dreams Publishing),
joint collection with Julie Maclean, 2016.

Indigo Dreams Publishing Ltd
24, Forest Houses
Cookworthy Moor
Halwill
Beaworthy
Devon
EX21 5UU
www.indigodreams.co.uk